What's It  Alphy?

Book 6

Easter Joy And Celebration

What's It All About, Alphy?

Book 6

Easter Joy And Celebration

Davo Roberts

Books written simply & clearly, to help you think, learn and grow!

pulp theology

USA & Canada - www.pulptheology.com

UK & Europe - www.pulptheology.co.uk

Acknowledgements

Text & Graphics Copyright © 2023 Dave G Roberts
Editing & Proofing: Roger Kirby

What's It All About, Alphy? Easter Joy And Celebration
Version 1.0
ISBN: 9798374792669
Also available in full colour on Kindle

Book 6 in the "What's It All About, Alphy?" Series

Previously released as Podcasts on the Partakers website:
http://www.partakers.co.uk
Parts of this book may have been published in other PulpTheology books.

Dedication

Firstly, to the Lord our God – Father, Son and Holy Spirit. I wouldn't be here without Him.

Secondly to my wife, Youngmi. She is my one and my only. I can't imagine life without her. I thank God for her daily.

Roger Kirby, who was mentor, editor, but most of all good friend. He fought the good fight and is now in the presence of His saviour, Jesus Christ.

How To Look Up The Bible

Contents

As We Begin

Easter. A time when the death and resurrection of the man known as Jesus Christ is remembered and commemorated worldwide.

In a lot of people's minds though, Easter doesn't have the same charm and allure as Christmas, when His birth is celebrated.

Perhaps that is, in part, due to people being more comfortable when confronted with a baby, than the death of a man.

To ease that discomfort we have Easter Eggs being delivered by the Easter Bunny. That is certainly true for those outside of the Church.

No other human birth in history causes more of the world to pause, take a breath and celebrate in different ways. The birth of Jesus Christ caused the world to change.

That is what the world celebrates at Christmas. The man that this baby would grow into, Jesus Christ, is the most talked about person in history. Almost everyone has an opinion about Him.

Yet, who was this man we know as Jesus Christ?

What did He do and what has He to do with us today, some 2,000 years after His birth?

When the human we know as Jesus Christ was born, His name imbued the very reason He was born.

His conception and birth were extraordinary at every level. Jesus was born to confirm God's promises, invite people into His Sonship.

Therefore revealing God as a loving Father, and to be our representative before Him.

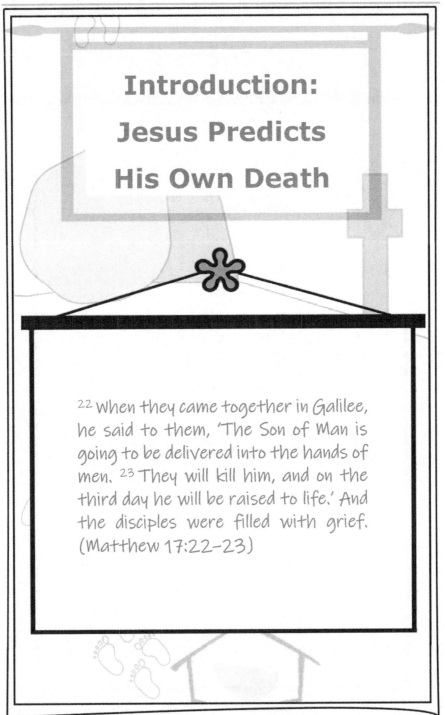

Introduction:
Jesus Predicts
His Own Death

22 When they came together in Galilee, he said to them, 'The Son of Man is going to be delivered into the hands of men. 23 They will kill him, and on the third day he will be raised to life.' And the disciples were filled with grief. (Matthew 17:22–23)

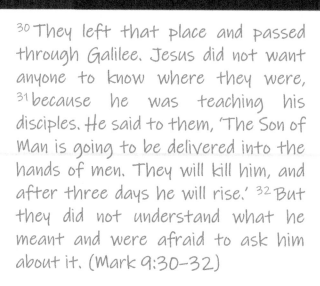

30 They left that place and passed through Galilee. Jesus did not want anyone to know where they were, 31 because he was teaching his disciples. He said to them, 'The Son of Man is going to be delivered into the hands of men. They will kill him, and after three days he will rise.' 32 But they did not understand what he meant and were afraid to ask him about it. (Mark 9:30–32)

While everyone was marvelling at all that Jesus did, he said to his disciples, 44 'Listen carefully to what I am about to tell you: the Son of Man is going to be delivered into the hands of men.' 45 But they did not understand what this meant. It was hidden from them, so that they did not grasp it, and they were afraid to ask him about it. (Luke 9:43b–45)

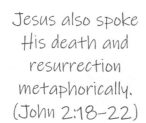

Jesus also spoke
His death and
resurrection
metaphorically.
(John 2:18–22)

We see this, when Jesus
compared His death and
resurrection to Jonah's
time in the belly of a fish.
(Matthew 12:40;
Matthew 16:4;
Luke 11:29–32)

Let's continue now, by
looking at the events
leading up to Jesus'
death on the cross.

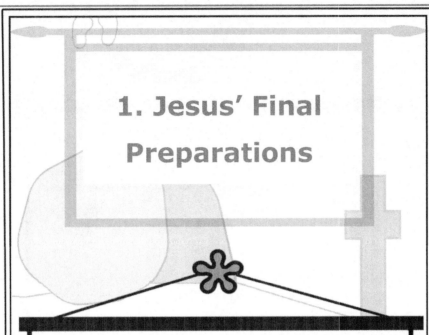

1. Jesus' Final Preparations

¹⁴ When the hour came, Jesus and his apostles reclined at the table. ¹⁵ And he said to them, 'I have eagerly desired to eat this Passover with you before I suffer. ¹⁶ For I tell you, I will not eat it again until it finds fulfilment in the kingdom of God.'

¹⁷ After taking the cup, he gave thanks and said, 'Take this and divide it among you. ¹⁸ For I tell you I will not drink again from the fruit of the vine until the kingdom of God comes.'

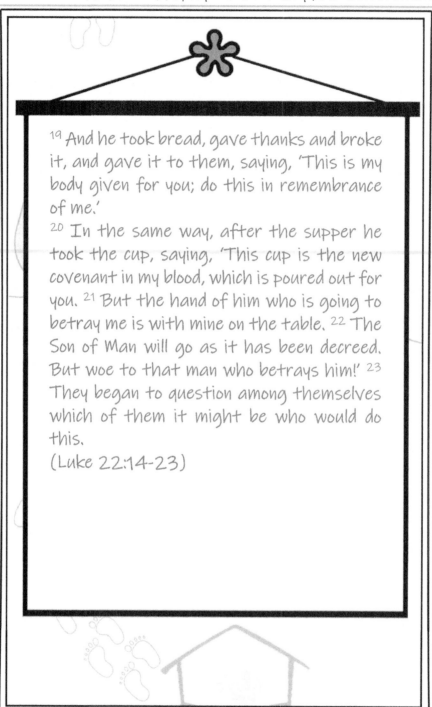

¹⁹ And he took bread, gave thanks and broke it, and gave it to them, saying, 'This is my body given for you; do this in remembrance of me.'

²⁰ In the same way, after the supper he took the cup, saying, 'This cup is the new covenant in my blood, which is poured out for you. ²¹ But the hand of him who is going to betray me is with mine on the table. ²² The Son of Man will go as it has been decreed. But woe to that man who betrays him!' ²³ They began to question among themselves which of them it might be who would do this.

(Luke 22:14-23)

The disciples needed a room within Jerusalem itself, and also required food - a lamb, bread, bitter herbs and wine.

The Passover meal contains historical and theological symbolism regarding the death of Jesus.

This is why this meal is the model for the central act of Christian worship, which we call Holy Communion.

Opening Prayer
First cup of wine
A dish of herbs and sauce
Story of the Passover recited
Psalm 113 was sung
Second cup of wine
Prayer of Grace
Main course of roast lamb with unleavened bread and bitter herbs
A further prayer
Third cup of wine.
Psalms 114 to 118 were then sung.
Fourth cup of wine.

This is what a typical Passover meal at the time of Jesus looked like.

Depending on your church, it can be called amongst other things, the Eucharist or The Lord's Supper.

As Christians, we are commanded to participate, by Jesus, our Lord: *"Do this in remembrance of me."* (Luke 22:19)

Some churches do it every service and others do it monthly.

Whenever we participate in it, we do it regularly as a remembrance of Jesus until He comes again! (1 Corinthians 11:26)

The bread symbolizes His body broken on the cross and the wine symbolizes His blood which was shed on the cross.

Therefore before we partake of the bread and wine, we are to examine ourselves and confess any unforgiven sin to Him. (1 Corinthians 11:28-29)

This is done because it would be hypocritical to eat it while harbouring known sin in our hearts and having fellowship with Jesus and others in the church!

It is here that we Christians spiritually feed upon Jesus Christ (1 Corinthians 11:24).

Therefore the Christian receive the benefits of this once and for all sacrifice in Jesus' death on the cross. (1 Corinthians 10:16)

This Holy Communion also represents the Christian's fellowship with other believers throughout the universal church. (1 Corinthians 10:17)

This Lord's Supper embodies the death of Jesus Christ for all sin (Luke 22:19) and our acceptance of His death for us.

As well as that, Jesus' death on the cross, epitomizes our dependence upon Him for all spiritual life and on Him alone.

As we remember, this makes it our own personal story. If something is only recalled as an historical event, then that is somebody else's story being recalled.

That is why this Holy Communion is personal. It is our story! It is my story. It is also your story if you are a Christian.

All these signify that the New Covenant made between God and the Christian, is a Covenant which guarantees salvation for the Christian believer.

The new covenant is a new meal, in order to remind Christians in every age, about the work of Jesus Christ on the Cross.

In this new covenant (Luke 22:20), Jesus claims that His death, was spoken about by the prophets Jeremiah and Ezekiel.

This is a new covenant in which God's people will be able to know God intimately. Why? Because all their sins will be forgiven.

Whenever a covenant was made between God and man in the Old Testament, the blood of an animal was always shed. This showed the cost of sin.

Jesus' blood, shed on the Cross, will be the seal on this New Covenant, which is why we remember it.

Since none of the disciples had done this, Jesus Himself undertakes the task. (John 13:4-5)

Peter is typically recalcitrant and resistant and objects (John 13:6, 8). Peter learns that only those cleansed by Jesus and trusting in Him fully, can be a part of the kingdom (John 13:7, 9).

As we look back at this episode, knowing what we do now of the Cross, we learn how this simple act of washing feet is symbolic of Jesus' sacrificial death on the Cross.

The Cross and the washing of feet are both displays of great love and service.

Just as Peter opposed Jesus going to the cross (Matthew 16:21-23), so he objected to having his feet washed here.

Jesus' getting up to serve symbolizes His coming to serve. As He took off his cloak, this symbolizes the taking off of His glory when He became man.

Jesus girding Himself with a towel, symbolizes his taking on human flesh in the incarnation at his birth.

As the water cleansed the feet, so Jesus death and blood cleanse from sin.

As He returned to where He was sitting and sat down after finishing this act of service, so did Jesus returned to the right hand of God after his work on the Cross.

When people become Christian, their sins are forgiven through Jesus' death on the Cross. That is when they had our "bath" as it were.

That is the very point when we, if we are Christians, were justified before God and we are declared His child. Having been justified already, we don't need a bath anymore!

But we do need the equivalent of a feet washing daily and or every time we take Holy Communion and a cleansing of our sin when we confess it before our God and repent.

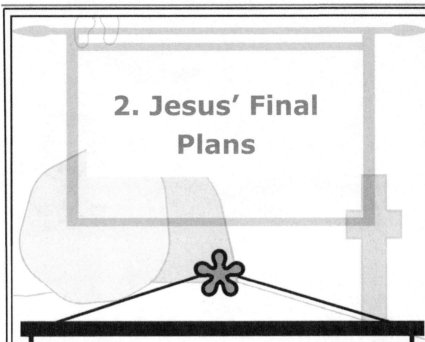

2. Jesus' Final Plans

¹ Now the Festival of Unleavened Bread, called the Passover, was approaching, ² and the chief priests and the teachers of the law were looking for some way to get rid of Jesus, for they were afraid of the people. ³ Then Satan entered Judas, called Iscariot, one of the Twelve. ⁴ And Judas went to the chief priests and the officers of the temple guard and discussed with them how he might betray Jesus. ⁵ They were delighted and agreed to give him money. ⁶ He consented, and watched for an opportunity to hand Jesus over to them when no crowd was present. (Luke 22:1-6)

Passover, Pentecost and Feast of Tabernacles were the three most important feasts on the Jewish calendar. (Leviticus 21)

All Jewish men were expected to visit Jerusalem. (Deuteronomy 16:16)

The Passover Feast was to commemorate the deliverance of Israel from Egypt (Exodus 11-12).

This was a time for remembering and greatly rejoicing.

Let's continue by comparing and contrasting the plans of Jesus, with those of His enemies.

Plans of Jesus

Jesus is in control
Plans the Passover meal (Luke 22:7-12)
The meal is part of His plan (Luke 22:16)
He knows Judas' plan (Luke 22:21-22)
Replaces the old leaders of God with His men
(Luke 22: 30)

Plans of Jesus' enemies

Plot to kill Jesus (Luke 22:2)
Arranges for Judas to betray Jesus
(Luke 22:3)
Satan's purpose is to destroy Jesus
(Luke 22:3, Luke 22:31)

All the elements in the plot conspiring against Jesus had been allowed for. The death of Jesus was no accident, writes Peter later in life.

"For you know that it was not with perishable things such as silver or gold that you were redeemed from the empty way of life handed down to you from your forefathers, but with the precious blood of Christ, a lamb without blemish or defect. He was chosen before the creation of the world, but was revealed in these last times for your sake. Through him you believe in God, who raised him from the dead and glorified him, and so your faith and hope are in God."
(1 Peter 1:18-21)

After Jesus' last prayers in Gethsemane, Judas fulfils his betrayal of Jesus with a kiss to identify Him and Jesus is arrested (Mark 14:45-46).

Jesus is taken away to be rejected by those closest to Him, to face trial, be whipped and crucified.

Jews were expected to remove all yeast from their houses (Exodus 12:15).

This was to serve as a reminder that their ancestors left Egypt in a hurry and had to eat bread without yeast.

Jesus had warned his disciples about the "yeast of the Pharisees, which is hypocrisy" (Luke 12:1).

In other words, the religious leaders had cleansed their houses but not their hearts.

The last thing the religious leaders wanted was a messianic uprising during Passover (Luke 19:11).

As for Judas, he was motivated and energized by satan (John 13:2, 27) and had never a true believer because his sins had never been cleansed by the Lord (John 13:10-11).

Therefore Judas had never believed or received eternal life (John 6:64-71).

However, Judas had been given authority and had been preaching the same message.

This shows how close a person can come to the kingdom of God and still be lost (Matthew 7:21-29)

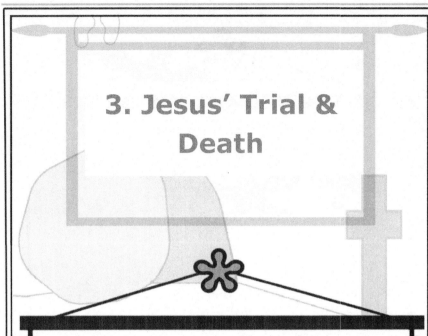

3. Jesus' Trial & Death

¹³ See, my servant will act wisely; he will be raised and lifted up and highly exalted. ¹⁴ Just as there were many who were appalled at him —his appearance was so disfigured beyond that of any human being and his form marred beyond human likeness —¹⁵ so he will sprinkle many nations, and kings will shut their mouths because of him.

For what they were not told, they will see, and what they have not heard, they will understand. (Isaiah 52:13-15)

¹⁰ Yet it was the Lord's will to crush him and cause him to suffer, and though the Lord makes his life an offering for sin,
he will see his offspring and prolong his days, and the will of the Lord will prosper in his hand.
¹¹ After he has suffered,
he will see the light of life and be satisfied;
by his knowledge my righteous servant will justify many, and he will bear their iniquities.
(Isaiah 53:10-11)

Following His betrayal, Jesus is now facing trial in a Roman court, being interrogated by Pontius Pilate.

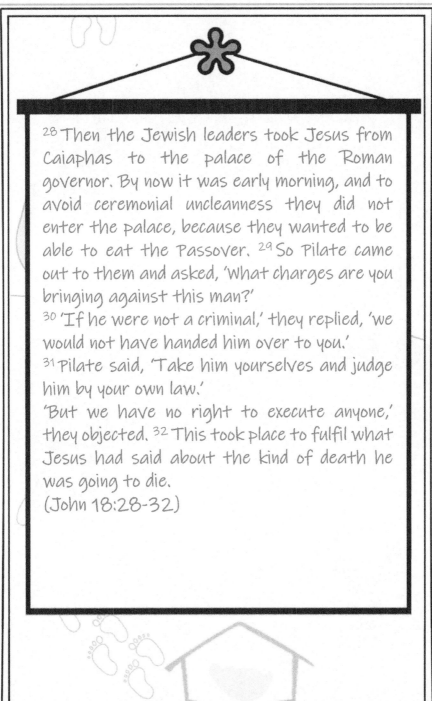

28 Then the Jewish leaders took Jesus from Caiaphas to the palace of the Roman governor. By now it was early morning, and to avoid ceremonial uncleanness they did not enter the palace, because they wanted to be able to eat the Passover. 29 So Pilate came out to them and asked, 'What charges are you bringing against this man?'

30 'If he were not a criminal,' they replied, 'we would not have handed him over to you.'

31 Pilate said, 'Take him yourselves and judge him by your own law.'

'But we have no right to execute anyone,' they objected. 32 This took place to fulfil what Jesus had said about the kind of death he was going to die.

(John 18:28-32)

Here we see that Jesus is before the Roman governor, Pontius Pilate.

Pilate gave in to Jesus' accusers and permitted the flogging and mockery in the hope of shaming Jesus' accusers (John 19:1-3).

Pilate affirmed Jesus' innocence after the scourging (John 19:4).

Jesus' refusal to answer, stung Pilate into reminding Jesus of his Roman authority (John 19:10).

Jesus, however, corrected Pilate's idea of authority and told him that although Pilate may have power on earth, Jesus' power reached beyond earth (John 19:11).

Jesus knew that his work of bring people back to God in a loving relationship did not rest on the actions of a mere Roman governor.

Pilate was more concerned with his own position than he was for justice.

In all this, we see Jesus as the true lamb of the Passover.

Jesus, bearing His own cross, was killed as a common criminal.

It was Pilate who was responsible for fixing the sign "The King of the Jews" upon Jesus' cross (John 19:19-22).

The clothes of condemned prisoners were given to soldiers on duty (John 19:23-24).

We see that even when He Himself was in agony, Jesus showed concern for his mother, committing her to the Apostle John (John 19:26-27).

The crucifixion site "was purposely chosen to be outside the city walls because the Law of Moses forbade such within the city walls.

We know from historical records, that for sanitary reasons, the crucified body was sometimes left to rot on the cross and serve as a disgrace, a convincing warning and deterrent to passers-by.

We also know from historical records, that sometimes the subject was eaten while alive and still on the cross by wild beasts.

As for Jesus, we know that His face was beaten beyond recognition. (Isaiah 52:14; Matthew 27:28-30)

The whipping of Jesus reduced His flesh to something like raw hamburger mince. The whips used had pieces of glass, metal and rocks stuck to the cord so as to inflict as much damage as possible.

Jesus had a crown of thorns pushed into his scalp (John 19:2), as a further act of mockery.

In Jesus' final moments before death, He uttered: "I am thirsty." (John 19:28) "It is finished." (John 19:30).

The desire of the Jewish leadership (John 19:32) to fulfil their rituals was important because the Sabbath fell within the Passover festival.

The breaking of Jesus' legs (John 19:32-33) sped up the process of His death. The piercing of Jesus' side, and the flow of blood and water proved Jesus was really dead (John 19:34).

Jesus was buried under the care of Joseph of Arimithea and Nicodemus. (John 19:38-39)

The significance of "*in which no-one had ever been laid*" (John 19:41) is to demonstrate that the body of Jesus at no point came into contact with the decay of a dead body.

But Jesus' death and burial is not the end. Oh no!

However, before we continue, we shall quickly investigate now what Jesus' death on a Roman cross two thousand years ago means for humanity today and why He had to die on a cross in the first place.

We continue by asking ourselves "What has Jesus' death done for all humanity, of all time?

All human beings, in their natural state, are born sinners and have rebelled against God (Romans 3:23).

However, because of Jesus' death on the cross God offers forgiveness (Ephesians 1:7), peace (Romans 5:1) and reconciliation with God, so that a person can choose to no longer be His enemy (2 Corinthians 5:19).

Through the cross of Jesus, and only through the cross, we are made just before God (Romans 3:24-26), it cleanses us from sin (1 John 1:7) and makes us right before Almighty God (2 Corinthians 5:21).

Because of Jesus Christ's death on a Roman cross, all those who follow Him have freedom from the power of slavery to sin (Galatians 5:1) and freedom from the power of the devil (Hebrews 2:14).

However, none of the above things are true if we do not choose to follow Jesus.

Are you following Jesus Christ and in relationship with God through Him?

4. Why Did Jesus Go To The Cross?

¹⁸ For you know that it was not with perishable things such as silver or gold that you were redeemed from the empty way of life handed down to you from your ancestors, ¹⁹ but with the precious blood of Christ, a lamb without blemish or defect. (1 Peter 1:18-19)

Sin is what separates humans from God and as a consequence leads to both a spiritual and physical death (Romans 3:23, Romans 6:23, Isaiah 59:2).

In the Old Testament, sins were dealt with by blood sacrifices of atonement as coverings for sin (Leviticus 17:11), for without the shedding of blood there can be no remission of sin (Hebrews 9:22).

A blood sacrifice is God's way of dealing with sin. These blood sacrifices of the Old Testament signified several things, as we shall see.

The blood sacrifice provided a covering for sin as it showed the great cost of sin. Think of it as an exchange or substitution.

The blood sacrifice of the Old Testament was only always going to be a temporary measure as it pointed forward to Jesus' death.

The permanent solution is not in continual animal sacrifice of the Old Testament because the blood of animals cannot take away sin but was only a veneer or covering (Hebrews 10:4).

If Jesus lacked either full divinity or full humanity, it would not be the full substitutionary sacrifice that was necessary to bear the permanent consequences of sin!

When Jesus died on the cross, he bore the consequences of all sin — past, present and future. Including our own.

Jesus therefore became sin for humanity (2 Corinthians 5:21) and it was His precious blood as a lamb without spot or blemish (1 Peter 1:18-19) that fulfils God's requirements permanently.

We remember that towards sin and sinful behaviour, God has great fury, anger and wrath (Jeremiah 21:5). Yet as we are also reminded, "He is slow to anger and quick to forgive". (Micah 7:18)

Propitiation is the turning aside of God's anger by the offering of the sacrifice of Christ.

God's anger and judgment of sin falls on Christ, instead of us.

Everybody needs to approach God to appease His anger, in order to accept it (Romans 3:25; Isaiah 53:5; John 2:2, 5:6).

What is more, not only was it propitiation, but also an act of redemption!
What is redemption, you may well be asking!

At the time of the New Testament, this word was used to refer to the buying back of a slave - the price paid to buy the slave's freedom.

God paid redemption so that humans can be freed from the slavery to sin (John 8:35 Romans 7:14).

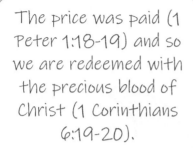

The price was paid (1 Peter 1:18-19) and so we are redeemed with the precious blood of Christ (1 Corinthians 6:19-20).

However, it is our responsibility to choose that way! God does not coerce forcefully. He leaves it as a choice for humans to make as individuals.

Have you made that decision for yourself? It is not too late!

As we look in the Gospel accounts, we see the temptations of Jesus by satan in the wilderness.

satan uses Peter to try and deflect Jesus away from the cross. satan used Judas to betray Jesus to the Romans.

If Jesus had ever succumbed to temptation, and sinned in thought, word, action or inaction, then He Himself would have needed a Saviour.

That is why Jesus is the perfect sacrifice – because He never sinned and always did what He saw God the Father wanting Him to

Jesus' death on the cross is the centrepiece of all human history and the focal point of eternity. At the cross, Jesus' mission is accomplished.

At the cross, this God-man, Jesus Christ paid the penalty for all sin of all time, so that people can have the opportunity to be restored into relationship with God.

Some people suggest that Jesus didn't die on the cross, but rather somebody was made to be His substitute. This is a lie of the devil.

Nobody could have been a substitute or the Jewish leaders would have said so when the rumours of Jesus' resurrection began to circulate.

The Romans kept strict discipline and regimen. Nobody would have been able to get in and somehow substitute themselves for Jesus. Yes, somebody else carried the cross for Him, but nobody but Jesus was nailed to that cross. Jesus died on that cross and not some substitute.

However, such is the enormity of the love of God, that each person has a choice to make – follow Jesus and take up your own cross and be an overcomer

A person can deny the cross and its meaning and when Jesus Christ comes again in judgment, they will find that He denies them entrance into His glorious kingdom.

How a person thinks of the cross of Jesus Christ, ultimately has relevance to them and affects their reality.

The cross, epitomises God's glory, and if there was any other way that He could restore people into relationship with Himself, surely He would have done it that way.

But there was no other way – Jesus Christ, simultaneously fully God and fully man, died on a Roman cross. He took on the sins of the world, paying the greatest price, so that people can be restored into relationship with God the Father.

That includes you and me. Have you made that choice for yourself?

The cross of Jesus Christ is amazing love in action and is ignored at great peril.

The wisdom of God, as exhibited on and in the Cross of Jesus Christ, is foolishness but only to those who don't accept it.

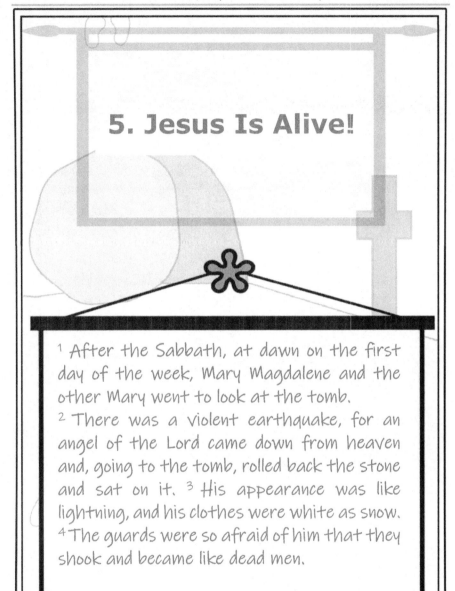

5. Jesus Is Alive!

¹ After the Sabbath, at dawn on the first day of the week, Mary Magdalene and the other Mary went to look at the tomb. ² There was a violent earthquake, for an angel of the Lord came down from heaven and, going to the tomb, rolled back the stone and sat on it. ³ His appearance was like lightning, and his clothes were white as snow. ⁴ The guards were so afraid of him that they shook and became like dead men.

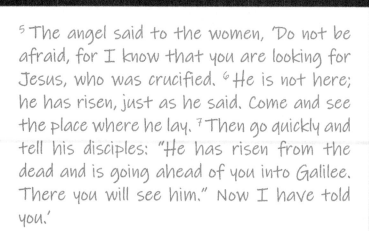

⁵ The angel said to the women, 'Do not be afraid, for I know that you are looking for Jesus, who was crucified. ⁶ He is not here; he has risen, just as he said. Come and see the place where he lay. ⁷ Then go quickly and tell his disciples: "He has risen from the dead and is going ahead of you into Galilee. There you will see him." Now I have told you.'

⁸ So the women hurried away from the tomb, afraid yet filled with joy, and ran to tell his disciples. ⁹ Suddenly Jesus met them. 'Greetings,' he said. They came to him, clasped his feet and worshipped him. ¹⁰ Then Jesus said to them, 'Do not be afraid. Go and tell my brothers to go to Galilee; there they will see me.' (Matthew 28:1-10)

Look at all the evidence for Jesus' tomb being empty! Look them up in your Bible.

Two Marys watch the burial of Jesus into the tomb (Matthew 27:61, Mark 15:47, Luke 23:54-55).

Roman soldiers guard the tomb and an official Roman seal is placed upon it (Matthew 27:62-66)

The women prepare burial spices for the body of Jesus and then they rest (Luke 23:56).

In the meant time, an angel rolls the stone away from the entrance to the tomb of Jesus (Matthew 28:2-4).

The women arrive at the tomb at dawn with spices (Matthew 28:1, Mark 16:1-4, Luke 24:1-3, John 20:1).

Some angels then appear to the women, telling them of the good news of Jesus rising from the dead and that Jesus is alive! (Matthew 28:5-7, Mark 16:5-7, Luke 24:4-8).

The women then run back to excitedly to tell the disciples (Matthew 28:8, Mark 16:8, Luke 24:9-11, John 20:2)

Peter and John speed off to investigate the empty tomb: (Luke 24:12, John 20:3-9)

Peter and John then return home having seen the empty tomb (Luke 24:12, John 20:10).

Mary Magdalene weeps by the empty tomb (John 20:11) She sees two angels sitting on the place where Jesus's body had been lying. (John 20:12-13)

These are historical facts for the bodily resurrection of Jesus Christ.

Look at the amazingly changed attitude of the disciples after seeing the risen Jesus. The disciples were like new people, changed from a group of defeated, cowardly people to victorious, brave people who rejoiced greatly.

If Jesus' body was still lying dead in the tomb, then both the Roman and Jewish authorities would have produced His dead body in order to quench the new movement. But they did not!

Nobody who could have produced the dead body of Jesus, did so. Their silence is as significant as the preaching of the Disciples.

The Jewish leaders certainly would have produce the body of Jesus if they could, as that would swiftly quell this new movement, as they started to lose people to the Church.

The survival, growth and impact of the early church is a great witness to the resurrection of Jesus Christ. If there was no bodily resurrection of Jesus' would people have risked persecution and death for a knowing lie?

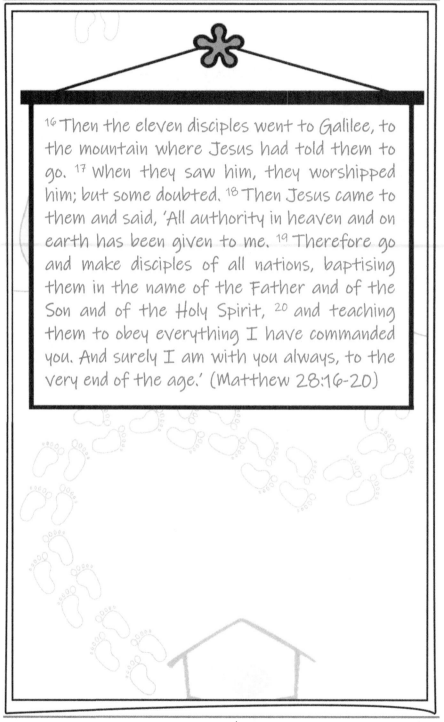

¹⁶ Then the eleven disciples went to Galilee, to the mountain where Jesus had told them to go. ¹⁷ When they saw him, they worshipped him; but some doubted. ¹⁸ Then Jesus came to them and said, 'All authority in heaven and on earth has been given to me. ¹⁹ Therefore go and make disciples of all nations, baptising them in the name of the Father and of the Son and of the Holy Spirit, ²⁰ and teaching them to obey everything I have commanded you. And surely I am with you always, to the very end of the age.' (Matthew 28:16-20)

Having been raised from the dead, Jesus' mission to earth is coming to an end and shortly He will be returning to the right hand of the Father.

Just as He had said to His disciples a few times before He went to His death on the cross.

Before He does leave though, He has some final instructions for His disciples.

However, during their last discussion with Jesus, the disciples were still expecting Him to lead a revolution against the Romans (Acts 1:6).

Despite all Jesus had said to them in the previous three years, the disciples still seemingly did not understand that Jesus had come to lead a spiritual kingdom and not a political kingdom.

Jesus commands that His disciples are to go and tell the world about what He has done, using His authority.

What do we know about Jesus' authority?

Throughout the Gospel of Matthew, Jesus' authority is a major theme.

Where Matthew records Jesus doing miracles, this is to highlight Jesus authority in action and not just merely in words.

Matthew records Jesus' authority to forgive sins (Matthew 9:6) and He imparted authority to his disciples for a short time when they went on a mission (Matthew 10).

Jesus has authority over all things, all people, all circumstances and happenings. Jesus has authority over all spiritual beings, whether angels or demons.

Jesus has authority over all nations, governments and rulers. Jesus has authority over all earthly and spiritual authorities. Jesus has the authority.

Through His death on the cross and His rising from the dead, Jesus has conquered all enemies.

How was this command to go to all the earth to be done by the Disciples? In the power of the Holy Spirit, who the disciples were told to wait for.

Jesus then physical ascends into the heavens (Mark 16:14-19; Luke 24:50-51 and Acts 1:1-12).

Even after Jesus had vanished into the clouds, the disciples still gathered around looking into the sky for Him to return. What were they thinking?

Could they not believe what they had just witnessed first-hand? Did they mis-hear what it was that Jesus had said quite clearly?

It was as if they still hadn't learnt obedience to Jesus' commands. Two angels appear to the disciples, saying:

"Men of Galilee,' they said, 'why do you stand here looking into the sky? This same Jesus, who has been taken from you into heaven, will come back in the same way you have seen Him go into heaven.'" (Acts 1:11)

The disciples then returned to Jerusalem and waited, just as they were told to do. They didn't have to wait long. Just ten days.

The early church exploded numerically as the disciples obeyed Jesus and exercised His authority and His power. You and I, if you are a Christian, are the results of the obedience of those disciples.

MeeWOW!

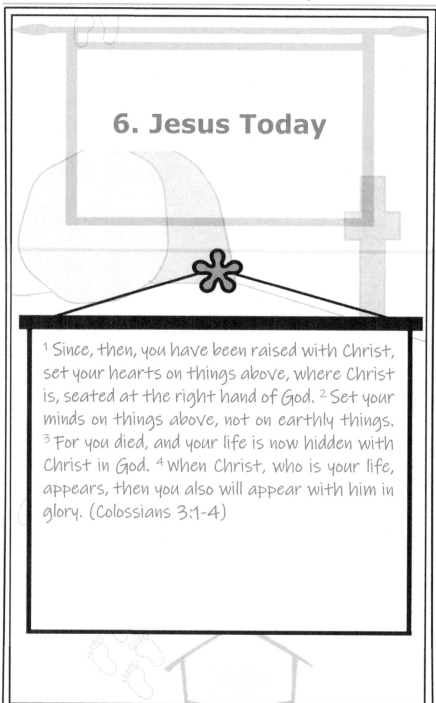

6. Jesus Today

¹ Since, then, you have been raised with Christ, set your hearts on things above, where Christ is, seated at the right hand of God. ² Set your minds on things above, not on earthly things. ³ For you died, and your life is now hidden with Christ in God. ⁴ When Christ, who is your life, appears, then you also will appear with him in glory. (Colossians 3:1-4)

As Christians, if we are listening, we are constantly being reminded by God the Holy Spirit, of our status before God.

The Holy Spirit, who lives within us, is always there behind us, reminding us, that we are now His children and not His enemy.

MeeWOW!

Therefore as Christians, we are to stop living as if we were His enemy. To help us, Paul tells of five marks of our identity as Christians.

Firstly, Christians have died with Jesus Christ (Colossians 3:3a)

Jesus not only died for us, but we died with Him. Christ not only died for sin, but died unto sin to break its power. Through the work of the Holy Spirit we are in Christ.

As Christians, we have died with Jesus Christ. Our new identity is Jesus Christ and we have died with Him.

MeeWOW!

Fourthly, Christians are hidden with Jesus Christ (Colossians 3:3b)

For those of you who like a good mystery, here is one for you. We are hidden with Him, for we no longer belong to this world, but we belong to Jesus Christ. We are hidden with Him in heaven, which means that our motives and strengths are to come from Him.

Our new identity is Christ and it is hidden with Him.

MeeWOW!

Lastly, Christians will be glorified with Jesus Christ (Colossians 3:4b)

When Jesus Christ comes again, we will see Him face to face. When He comes again, He will take us home. We shall enter eternal glory. We will not be hidden with Christ forever. When Christ is revealed in glory, we too shall be revealed in glory.

We have some of this glory now. One day the full extent of this glorification will be revealed. Our new identity is Christ, and we will be glorified with Him.

MeeWOW!

These five facts cover all three tenses in time - past, present and future.

In the past, we died and were raised with Christ. In the present, we live with Christ and we are hidden with Him.

In the future, when He comes again, we will be glorified with Him. **MeeWOW!**

However, until that time, Jesus still meets with people at the present time.

How does He do this?

Jesus walks with Christians, wherever we go and in particular in the darkest periods of our life. Jesus walks with those who proclaim to be following Him.

Jesus speaks whenever the Bible is faithfully preached and read from, just as He opened the eyes of those on the Emmaus road when He explained the Scriptures (Luke 24:27).

Jesus meets the Christian in the Communion or Lord's Supper, with the bread and wine, which symbolise His flesh and blood as an act of remembrance of what He did for humanity.

If you want to turn to God, there is no need for delay. He is ready and willing to take you as His own – right now. You only have to ask Him to forgive you and He will!

Being a Christian is a partnership between God and yourself. Deciding to change course in mid-life, is what is called conversion, being born again, or deciding to be a Christian.

When you place your faith in Jesus, becoming utterly dependent upon Him, you turn to God.

Once you have made that decision, you leave behind your rebellion against Him. As you live each day, becoming more involved with Jesus day by day, you will find yourself changing.

You stop doing things which separated you from Him and find yourself doing things that develop your relationship with Him.

Until you enter into that relationship, sin, or that which alienates you from God, controls your rebellion against Him in your attitudes and your activities.

You develop this relationship by allowing God to take control of your life, as He asks you to accept His management and guidance of your life.

God's point of view and His strength will become your point of view and your source of strength. You turn your mind, will and heart to Him for all you do.

If you want to make that decisive step and become a Christian, there are some simple steps to take.

Firstly, admit that you have done wrong against God and His ways and turn away from those attitudes.

Secondly, believe and trust in Jesus as your Saviour from the consequences of the anger of God towards you and your tendency to sin.

Call on Him, receive, trust, obey and worship Him, recognizing Him for who He is and what He has done.

Lastly, accept the Holy Spirit of God into your life as the major motivating force for all that you do.

Once sin has been confessed, Jesus is believed in and trusted as Saviour and the Holy Spirit has entered your life, then you are a Christian.

All these things happen together in a flash as you turn to God. Now you are ready to grow in grace and knowledge of our Jesus. Welcome to the family of God! God has chosen you; Jesus has paid for you and has put his mark within you through his Spirit (Ephesians 1:1-13).

Other
"What's It All About, Alphy?"
Books

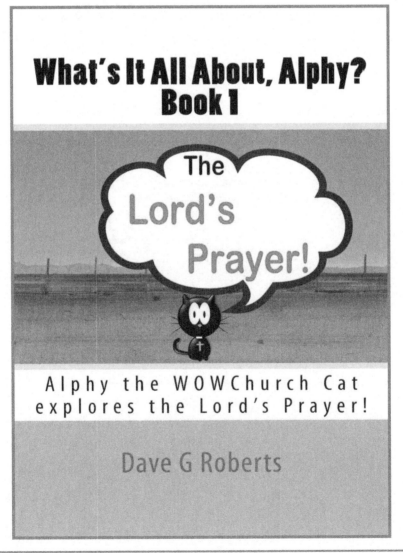

What's It All About, Alphy?
Book 1

The Lord's Prayer!

Alphy the WOWChurch Cat
explores the Lord's Prayer!

Dave G Roberts

Davo Roberts

The Surprise of Grace

Exploring Romans 5

Davo Roberts

The Christian in Days of Challenge

What's It All About Alphy?
Alphy Looks Into Romans 8

What's It All About Alphy?
Armoured For The Fight

The Christian Has Spiritual Armour

Davo Roberts

What's It All About Alphy?

5. Mary And The Magnificat

Davo Roberts

Other Books By This Author

AGOG: A Glimpse of God

An Ambassador in God's Orchestra of Joy

Dear Christian – Get A Good Grip

Dear Church: Wake up!

Developing Intimacy With God: A Little Book of 95 Prayers

Easter Essentials

Engaged In Battle

Exploring The Bible

God Gets His Hands Dirty

God, Internet Church & You

God's Two Words For You : Jesus and the Bible.

Helping the Forgotten Church

Heroes And Heretics Abound – History of the Church

Intimacy with God: The Christian Devotional Life

Living Life Right: Studies in Romans 12

Scriptural Delights: Exploring Psalm 119

When Love Hits Town

WOW Words of the Bible

Glimpses Into Series:

Leviticus: A Book Of Joy
1 & 2 Chronicles: Books of heritage And history
Psalms: A Book Of Life
Ezekiel: A Book Of Symbols And Visions.
The Gospels: Books Of Good News
Acts: A Book Of Action
Romans: A Book Of Freedom

Read This Book Series:

Volume 1: God Of The Bible
Volume 2: Jesus Christ
Volume 3: Being A Christian
Volume 4: The Church
Volume 5: Evangelism
Volume 6: The Christian Devotional Life

All books are available in Paperback and Kindle at:
PulpTheology.co.uk
PulpTheology.com

And all Amazon sites

About the Author

I was born in a small country town about 300 miles north east of Sydney in Australia. I was raised to be a sceptic cum agnostic cum atheist with the words "Churches are dangerous places" and this is like 30 years before Dawkins and His ilk uttered the words! Coming into my teenage years in the eighties, I decided if they are so dangerous let's go for a bit of danger!

So, I rebelled, became a Christian and started attending a local Christian youth group. After a bit, it was thought by my family that I was being brainwashed, so I was stopped from going for a couple of years, until I met somebody who I used to go to school with who invited me to her church, and I restarted from there.

As to how I came to the UK! Well, I came here from Australia for 6 months' travel around Europe! Or so I thought! That was in 1990! I view it as God having a sense of humour. He knows I don't like rain, cold and in particular - together! He has even given me the most beautiful of women as a wife, but she doesn't like hot weather! God sure has a sense of humour! In 2003, I had a minor stroke and I view that as God giving me a clip round the ear to stop being stubborn and to listen to Him for direction. I took redundancy from my career and went off to Moorlands College where I graduated in 2007 with a BA Th App (Hons).

I set up Partakers in 2007. I had recorded some audio files as part of a block placement during my 3rd year at Moorlands. Six months later I looked back on the site and discovered that the 16 audio files had been downloaded several thousand times, mainly in a country where evangelical Christians are persecuted. It was also part of my dissertation investigating if a Virtual Church could be part of the universal church. I based my study on the Church being one, holy, catholic and apostolic.

To date the Partakers Podcasting site has had about 7,000,000 unique visitors so far and about 10,000,000 downloads. The Partakers YouTube site has had over 2,000,000 viewings. Combined, there is a reach of over 100 nations annually. Overall, I also have over 100 different contributors globally including several people from the church we are attached to and helping all to practice their gifting.

As for the name Partakers, I got the idea straight from Matthew 5:6, which I paraphrase as "Blessed are those who partake after righteousness for they will be filled." I have an accountability team set up by the church we attend, for mentoring, prayer, guidance, advice and accountability. I also have people on Facebook to keep an eye on what I say and do, to help ensure that those things are within biblical confines.

Peace and blessings

Davo Roberts

About Partakers & PulpTheology

Vision Statement: Partakers exists to communicate and disseminate resources for the purposes of Christian Discipleship, Evangelism and Worship by employing radical and relevant methods, including virtual reality and online distribution.

Mission Statement: Helping the world, one person at a time, to engage in whole life discipleship, as Partakers of Jesus Christ.

info@partakers.co.uk
www.partakers.co.uk

Printed in Great Britain
by Amazon

24096540R00069